BEGINNERS GUIDE TO THE STOCK MARKET

*The Simple **Step by Step** Guide for Investing in Stocks, Building Your Wealth and Creating a Long-Term Passive Income*

JAMIE THOMSON

Beginners Guide to the Stock Market

© COPYRIGHT 2020 THE LIFE GRADUATE PUBLISHING GROUP
ALL RIGHTS RESERVED.

The content contained within this book may not be reproduced, duplicated or transmitted without direct written permission from the author or the publisher.

Under no circumstances will any blame or legal responsibility be held against the publisher, or author, for any damages, reparation, or monetary loss due to the information contained within this book. Either directly or indirectly.

Legal Notice:

This book is copyright protected. This book is only for personal use. You cannot amend, distribute, sell, use, quote or paraphrase any part, or the content within this book, without the consent of the author or publisher.

Disclaimer Notice:

Please note the information contained within this document is for educational and entertainment purposes only. All effort has been executed to present accurate, up to date, and reliable, complete information. No warranties of any kind are declared or implied. Readers acknowledge that the author is not engaging in the rendering of legal, financial, medical or professional advice. The content within this book has been derived from various sources. Please consult a licensed professional before attempting any techniques outlined in this book.

By reading this document, the reader agrees that under no circumstances is the author responsible for any losses, direct or indirect, which are incurred as a result of the use of the information contained within this document, including, but not limited to, — errors, omissions, or inaccuracies.

To those of you that are life learners, take daily action and make decisions now, that will have a positive and long-term impact on your financial wealth.

TABLE OF CONTENTS

INTRODUCTION   1

CHAPTER 1   7

THE 7 MONEY GUIDING PRINCIPLES FOR WEALTH CREATION

CHAPTER 2   19

ESTABLISH YOUR FINANCIAL GOALS

- THE 8 KEY STEPS TO ESTABLISH YOUR FINANCIAL GOALS

CHAPTER 3   30

THE STRATEGY TO STOCK MARKET INVESTING

- STRETCH BEFORE YOUR SPRINT
- WHAT CAN IMPACT GLOBAL MARKETS?

CHAPTER 4   36

BEGINNER STOCK MARKET TERMINOLOGY TO KNOW

- COMMON STOCK MARKET TERMS

CHAPTER 5   49

QUICK TIPS TO SAVE YOU MONEY

- THE 7 TIPS TO SAVE YOU MONEY FOR INVESTING

CHAPTER 6 — 54

HOW TO INVEST IN STOCKS

- HOW TO MAKE MONEY IN STOCKS
- HOW DO I PURCHASE STOCKS?
- WHAT IS DOLLAR COST AVERAGING?
- USING STOP LOSS ORDERS

CHAPTER 7 — 77

THE 7 RULES FOR STOCK SELECTION FOR BEGINNERS

CHAPTER 8 — 83

INVESTMENT AUTOMATION AND WEALTH ACCELERATION

- BUILDING YOUR STOCK BUILDING WEALTH SYSTEM

CHAPTER 9 — 91

STOCK MARKET MISTAKES BEGINNERS MAKE

CHAPTER 10 — 97

21 GREAT MONEY TIPS TO GROW YOUR WEALTH AND PASSIVE INCOME

CHAPTER 11 — 101

DEVELOPING YOUR STOCK INVESTMENT PLAN

CONCLUSION — 106

RESOURCES — 113

INTRODUCTION

The Stock Market can be a fantastic way to invest and earn a long-term passive income, but where do you start? What needs to be done to set-up an account to purchase your first stock and importantly, what should you buy? You don't want to lose your money, but you also understand the importance of making your money work for you rather than just sitting idle in the bank. People tell you all the time that the stock market is risky. But is that true? Is it a good time to buy now or should you wait?

These are just some of the questions that the 'Beginners Guide to the Stock Market' will answer and get you started on your financial journey.

"It's not supposed to be easy. Anyone who finds it easy is stupid."
Charlie Munger, American Investor and Philanthropist

Misconceptions

The images that people see and the misconceptions people have about the stock market include fast cars, get-rich-quick schemes, stock booms, stock crashes, bull & bear markets, quick cash, insider trading and panic buying and selling are just few that come to mind. Unfortunately, many 'should' be investing in the stock market but never take action to do so because of these clouded misconceptions.

On the flip side, there are so many that would *love* to invest their money in the stock market but usually come up against the following five concerns or fears.

1. They don't know where to start. It all seems too complicated!
2. They hear that the stock market is 'too risky' and are afraid to invest.
3. They unsure how *much* to invest, *where* to invest and *when* to invest.
4. They have invested before; have lost their money and are cautious about trying again.
5. There is too much terminology to understand.

The 'Beginners Guide to the Stock Market' is all about understanding how the stock market works, learning some terminology basics, wealth-building strategies, great stock investing habits, automating your stock investments, creating a passive income and investing your money wisely for the long-term. It brings together all of the information you will need to know to get started and importantly, keeping it condensed into approx. 90 minutes of reading or listening.

This is certainly not a Financial Planning or Stock Trader's textbook, nor will it contain any unethical tips or tricks or 'get rich quick' schemes. This book will provide you with a very sound, practical, common sense and straight forward approach for the best way to invest in the Stock Market and how to get started with the best chance of success for your investment future.

It is essential to note from the outset that this is a 'Beginners Guide', and although it does provide the basics, I will show you how to create an excellent source of long-term passive income and establish your financial and wealth goals. This book will also demonstrate that you don't need a huge income or to be across the markets every day to become a millionaire from purchasing stocks, in fact, I will show you a straight forward savings and investment strategy that with time and the power of compounding interest, you can achieve massive returns. It will be an excellent starting platform for you to improve your financial position, start your stock investment journey or continue with a few tweaks and changes. Yes, it is possible to make money quickly, but it is not as simple as many would have you believe. I don't want to discourage your appetite from making quick money, but you should be aware of the basics:

- *Learn the basic knowledge, skills and terminology first.*
- *Undertake professional and specialized training.*
- *Invest the time and become disciplined and committed to master the trade.*

If you already have money to invest, or you are just about to embark on your journey with no savings at all, I will provide examples and action tasks for you to start the process and share with you the essentials of investing in the stock market. Note: I use 'invest' as opposed to 'trading' because they are two very distinct ways of approaching the stock market. Trading implies short term buying and selling as opposed to 'investing' that has a longer-term perspective.

Your First Steps

For many years, I have been investing in the stock market, and along the way, my 'beginner mistakes' have taught valuable lessons that have both been challenging but critical for my journey. Without these lessons, I wouldn't be in the fantastic financial position I am now, earning many thousands of dollars in passive income, no matter if I'm sleeping or awake. Importantly, this book will also show you how to automate your finances so you can use the set-and-forget approach with just 30-minute quarterly checks to ensure everything is tracking as intended.

Finally, this book will help you to establish the right 'Money Mindset' with the best financial and money guiding principles that will position you well for the years to come. It will help you to manage your money more wisely, invest it sensibly, and allow you to have more control over how you build your wealth.

With that, I think it is the perfect time to start your stock investment journey and learn what it takes to do well in the stock market.

"Someone's sitting in the shade today because someone planted a tree a long time ago."
Warren Buffett

Chapter One

The 7 Money Guiding Principles for Wealth Creation

Right from the outset and before you start investing in the Stock Market, you must have a set of Guiding Principles that will help to provide the structure you need for long-term investment thinking. These 7 Steps will form the backbone for your future investment strategy, and they will keep you on a path for great money management.

Financial Guiding Principle #1
Financial Goals

Investing in the Stock Market isn't about having some money, choosing a stock and then crossing your fingers hoping that you will someday become RICH! You need to have clarity on what your end financial goal will ideally look like and have an ongoing commitment for taking action. This all starts with developing your financial goals.

I credit my success to the **8 Key Steps** to establish my Financial Goals:

STEP 1. CLARITY
Dream Big. Get clarity on your ultimate financial goals.

STEP 2. PERSONAL
Make your financial goals personal and relevant to you.

STEP 3. TAKE ACTION
Take immediate action and write up your BIG financial goals.

STEP 4. PLAN
Develop your plan and course of actions steps.

STEP 5. TIME
Develop specific and realistic time frames for your goals.

STEP 6. COMMITMENT
Follow through with your commitment and start.

STEP 7. OPPORTUNITY
Be observant of opportunities that present.

STEP 8. START
Do not procrastinate. Get started today and take action.

Financial Guiding Principle #2

Develop Your Plan

The development of a plan will provide you with direction, and this will ensure that the decisions you make are in alignment with the strategy you have decided to pursue.

That's fine in theory, but what does a good financial plan look like and how do you develop one? Each plan will depend on your personality, if you are a risk-taker and importantly, your stage in life and what you want to achieve.

Teen to Early 20's – *Example Plan*

- I wish to complete my school studies and complete an internship
- I will continue to live at home for 2 – 3 years and get a casual job and save $50 p/week to invest in stocks. Once that amount accumulates to $500 every ten weeks, I will invest this as part of my wealth-building strategy.
- I will read 1 x book a month on investing to improve my knowledge.

It is expected that when someone is in their teens, they may not have a long-term view over a period greater than 2 – 3 years. Shorter and more specific plans are important, so you can build confidence, and you see more immediate results for 'wins on the board'.

A couple with or without young children – *Example Plan*

- We will increase our savings & investment plan to $100 per week. Every five weeks, we will invest $500 to grow our stockholding.

- We will continue with additional mortgage repayments on our home with a plan to pay off the mortgage in 10 years.

- We will provide the best education we possibly can for our children

- We plan to be financially independent by age 60 or earlier.

It is important that when you develop your plan that you think long-term. The great thing about a plan is that you will have more of a reason to stick and remain with it rather than having no financial plan at all. Your objectives will be clear, you have clarity on what you want to achieve, and you can structure your financials accordingly.

As a guide, remember to include the following:
- Your Objectives
- Your Budget (we will talk about this more later)
- Your current financial position
- Your timeline

Financial Guiding Principle #3
Take Control – Develop a Budget

Don't ever think that you need to be an accountant to establish a budget! Usually, a budget sounds boring, but what if I told you that you could become RICH by having a budget! Would that change your way of thinking?

Having a budget allows you to be clear about where you are directing your money for stock investment. If you have no budget, it is similar to having a bucket full of holes and every time you top the bucket up with water; it just spirts out.

The reason why I strongly encourage a budget is that you can allocate money first towards growing your wealth through investing. For example, if your Budget allocated $100 p/week towards purchasing stocks, you would have $1,200 every three months to invest. If you don't assign money via a budget, that $1,200 is highly likely to be spent on miscellaneous items that are liabilities rather than assets.

What is a liability and an asset?
Liabilities – Things that go down in value
Assets – Things that grow in value.

Financial Guiding Principle #4

Develop a supportive Habit Investment System.

Developing supportive investment habits will be a critical Guiding Principle for growing your wealth and your passive income. There are many supportive habits that I would encourage you to implement as part of your growth strategy. One key to habit development is to introduce your supportive habits incrementally and not all at once. For example, if you wanted to invest $50 p/week, just start with $10 and build that by only $2.00 per week. Yes, it will take you a further 20 weeks (5 months) to build to $50, however, by building up this savings habit slowly, you will become adjusted to the change without even seeing the difference, and your spending habits will very easily adjust. If you try and introduce a $50 p/week savings habit immediately, you are likely to be impacted within the first 2 – 3 weeks and then just STOP as it's not working out. Think of the incremental change as a 'Long-Term' viewpoint, because in 3 years when you have a fantastic savings plan, the slow build over 4 – 5 months will equate to nothing compared to what will happen if you give up after four weeks with nothing to show for it.

3 Financial Habit Tips

#1. Save little and save often

Example: $1 per day from age 18 to 65 would be worth approx. $400,000 thanks to the magic of compound interest. Even if you put in place a saving plan regardless of your age of $10 p/day for five years, it would be worth approx. $25,000!

#2. Automate a Savings Plan

Set up an automatic transfer in your Savings Account that occurs every 1 or 2 weeks. If it is automated, you don't need to think about it and your' investment savings' will grow thanks to the wonder of banking automation. We will discuss this later in the book.

#3. Asset or Liability

Each time you purchase something, consider if the purchase is an 'Asset' or a 'Liability'. Will this item be worth more in 5 years than it is now? Purchasing a new T.V. – No! Buying new designer shoes – NO! Investing in a great company with an excellent track record of growth – History tells us…YES!

Financial Guiding Principle #5

Become Comfortable with the Ups and Downs of the Stock Market

Understand from the very beginning that the Stock Market will rise and fall. It could shoot up very quickly, but it may also plummet dramatically. Again, take a long-term approach, hence why you take your time to invest in the right stocks, so you have confidence knowing that they will rebound to higher prices over time.

Investing is also a mental game, not just a financial one. You need to avoid the noise of the newspapers and the 'doomsday' merchants that prey on fear. **T.I.P**. If you want to lose money fast, sell when everyone is selling or panicking and buy when you are getting stock tips at parties when the market is flying!

Financial Guiding Principle #6
Invest in your growth

There is no greater investment you can make than in your personal growth. If you work hard at something for long enough, you will begin to master the skill and become extremely good at it. If you have an interest in investing, read more books, attend seminars by trusted and experienced professionals and learn the craft. It may be an initial cost at the beginning but think of it as an investment into your future.

Financial Guiding Principle #7
Commitment

One word will quickly determine if you will become a great investor or a mediocre one! COMMITMENT. You need to transition from being a motivated investor to a committed investor that will continue to learn, save, study the market, apply your knowledge and then invest. Only then will you see high financial returns and an ongoing passive income. Remember, all the work you put in now will flood back in returns later.

Chapter 2

Establish Your Financial Goals

The #1 Financial Guiding Principle mentioned in Chapter One was regarding setting the right financial goals. Here, I will expand in further detail and note the right mindset that you need to develop to become successful at investing.

The 8 Key Steps to establish your Financial Goals:

STEP 1. CLARITY
Dream Big. Get clarity on your ultimate financial goals.

Clarity is the number one step you need when establishing financial goals.
The first stage of financial goal setting should involve visualizing and what you want to achieve. The power of visualization is not to be underestimated. Seeing yourself as someone capable and ready for financial success creates an inner motivation to strive for your goals and dreams and promotes positive thinking, which will help you stay on track for success. It has also been

found to teach your brain to recognize what resources it will require to help you succeed in reaching your goals so that you are always seeking new opportunities.

The financial goals you settle on will need to be significant enough to drive you closer to your destination every day, and you cannot accomplish much if your goals are as average as getting a few cents extra as a raise.

Wealth goals are ways to improve your financial situation and achieve security and comfort rather than money-related anxiety. They should focus on not only liquid assets like money in your bank account but also non-liquid assets like your housing situation.

Consider the following questions when setting your wealth goals.
- Where do I want to be living?
- What investments do I want to own?
- How much money would it take to be living comfortably?
- What passive income can I generate, so my

money is 'working for me'?
- Is there a savings or financial goal I want to achieve?

STEP 2. PERSONAL
Make your financial goals personal and relevant to you

Your financial goals need to matter, and they need to matter to you. To establish a real drive to invest, your financial goals need to be ones that you are personally invested in. Think of the reasons why achieving a specific financial goal would make you happy and what it would allow you to do. Ask yourself, "what positive impact will it have for me?" Consider how it may help those around you whom you care about as well. Setting and achieving your financial goals requires making an ongoing commitment to invest.

STEP 3. TAKE ACTION
Take immediate action and write up your BIG goals

Once you've dreamed up your financial goals, the next step is to take immediate action. Now is not the time for procrastinating and dragging your feet. You must start today to see any change in your life. Even if you don't think you can accomplish any big steps right away, start with the small things and work your way up.

Start by gathering the necessary information and then begin implementing the newfound knowledge and resources, starting with the easy to implement and working your way up to the harder things. The momentum you gain from completing even the simplest of tasks will carry you through to tackling the bigger challenges. If you hesitate and allow your momentum to fade without taking action, you could jeopardize your chances of long-term financial success. If you have been guilty of procrastinating before, use this moment and change your financial path.

Write Your Financial Goals Down

Taking action begins with writing your financial goals down and reminding yourself of them regularly. The process of writing your goals down is like entering into an agreement with yourself. Think of it like writing out a contract in which you identify what you want to achieve and the date by which you want to achieve it by. Having agreed to this contract, you are now accountable for fulfilling it. You must take action to follow through on the contract and keep your promises to yourself.

Initially, choose financial goals that will be achievable within the given time limit. Even if they require a good deal of commitment, they will give you the confidence and strong foundation to begin working towards your overarching ten-year financial goals. This way, each goal you achieve will carry you closer to your long-term goals for much bigger successes, and the compounding effect will pay 'dividends'.

STEP 4. PLAN
Develop your plan and course of actions steps

Plotting the course for achieving your financial goals is a bit like being a ship captain voyaging into treacherous and unknown seas. Without careful planning and a way to chart your course, you risk running aground or getting lost at sea. However, so long as you take the proper precautions to plan out your financial journey, you can avoid the most unforeseen circumstances.

Developing your plan is a vital element for achieving any wealth-generating goal. Without knowing how to arrive at your financial goal, how will you know what you need to do to get there? Understanding each step allows you to implement the support money habits and actions that will bring you closer to success. Proper planning ensures that the actions you spend your time and effort on really matter and each one aids you in getting where you want to go.

How to Chart Your Financial Course

Many people falter in financial goal setting because they believe that simply writing their goals down is enough. They set the goals aside without any more in-depth thought, and as a result, they forget about them. This is a sure-fire way to significantly limit your opportunities and muddy the waters of your path to success. The best way to counteract this "set and forget" tendency is to thoroughly plan out the route you will take to reach your goal.

Your plan will depend on the size and difficulty of your financial goal. A short-term goal may only require five steps, while a stretch goal may involve 20. It may also involve some initial steps of automating your financials so you can develop a savings plan that you know you can achieve over a certain period.

STEP 5. TIME
Develop specific and realistic time frames for your goals

Set a specific timeline for each financial goal you plan to achieve. By setting a date by which a goal must be accomplished, you can begin to apply the timeframe to each step in the process.

Long-Term and Short-Term Timelines

There are a few differences in setting deadlines for short-term goals versus more involved goals. Those that can be accomplished in less than a year should be somewhat more in-depth with each part of the process having its own timeline and steps, as you have a reasonably accurate idea of what your life will look like at each stage of the process. Try to shift your deadlines as little as possible. For more long-term financial goals, such as those that you assign a five year or greater deadline to, focus on the smaller goals that will help you achieve the larger ones. You can adjust your long-term timelines when necessary as you go, as a lot is likely to change over the course of five years. Set yourself up for future success by concentrating on what you can achieve in the short-term.

STEP 6. COMMITMENT
Follow through with your commitment and start

Make the commitment to achieving your financial goals official and begin putting in the actual work to get things done. Everything you have done up to this moment has been preparatory work that will help you succeed during this step. Taking the plunge and moving forward with your goals will put you on the express path to financial success. Not everyone takes this first step, but most people who reach the implementation phase and make the commitment to following their carefully laid plans have an incredibly high chance of achieving their goals so long as they stay the course and see it through to the end.

This is the time to begin implementing the supportive daily financial habits that build the system and structures that will significantly increase your chances of success.

STEP 7. OPPORTUNITY
Be observant of opportunities that present

Opportunities are always passing by, but it's up to each of us to recognize and seize them. If you don't take an opportunity, it will be passed onto someone else, and you will miss out on whatever benefit it would have given you. To be sure you take full advantage of opportunities, you must be aware of them at all times. Frequently checking your financial goals and committing them to memory will help your subconscious recognize chances to further your progress when they appear.

STEP 8. START
Do not procrastinate. Get started today and take action.

The final phase of setting your financial goals is to act right now. You've established a plan and put in the preparatory work to complete the seven prior goal setting steps. Now it is time to actually go out and achieve those goals. There is no better time to start than today.

Chapter 3

The Strategy to Stock Market Investing

We all agree that our **#1** objective is to make as much money as we can from the stock market. It's why we invest both our time and hard-earned money and why you first need to understand the Five Key Rules that will accelerate your chances of generating great financial returns when you do it the right way.

You will never be able to pick the bottom or the very top of the market. There are just too many influencing factors out of your control to know exactly where the bottom of the market will fall or when we have reached the peak. If you do try, you are not an 'investor' you are simply a 'punter'. Don't get 'analysis paralysis' and try to complete such in-depth research on a particular company by reading stock broking reports and trying to develop a sophisticated accounting process. Unless you are an expert in the field and have spent many years as an analyst, an in-depth 50-page dossier is not required.

The key is to develop a long-term investment strategy with periodical investments that will build your stock portfolio over time.

1. Look for value, ignore the hype and buy with confidence.
2. Embrace market falls. Stocks are now 'On Sale'!

Stretch Before You Sprint

Having been an elite athletics runner in my junior years, I understand the huge importance of technique, stretching, training, jogging and then hitting top speed. The same components need to be applied to your stock market strategy.

Technique: Gain the knowledge and learn the techniques that the most successful investors implement. Try and emulate what they do and understand why their techniques have been so successful. Read books, listen and attend courses and gain some great basics to the stock market.

Stretching: Some may like to use Stock Market simulators to start with, but for some, the best experience can be by starting with a very small investment. 'Stretch' your investment muscles but tipping your toe in the water and get started. Get used to pressing the 'BUY' button.

Training: Slowly build your experience and knowledge by practicing what you have learnt to a larger scale. No amount of simulation practice will allow you to experience the real thing, so start small, build more confidence with each trade and get ready for bigger trades.

Jogging: Start to implement your investment strategy as per your investment plan and develop strong and supportive financial habits and a rhythm you can accommodate.

Hitting Top Speed: You are now ready to build your investment momentum to full speed. You have now completed all the preparation and training, and you are ready to hit full speed on your wealth creation and passive income strategy.

What impacts the market and why you just flow with the market 'river.'

There are so many factors that impact the movements of the market on a daily basis that you must learn to ignore the majority of them and just feel comfortable to 'float' with the stock market river. As with all starting streams, they eventually end up feeding into the big open waters where you will be free to paddle where you please. To begin with, you need to have an understanding that you can't control the world markets, but you can control the way you think about them. Historically, even following world wars and even the worst of economic depressions, the economy has recovered to greater heights.

Here is a small list of some of the factors that can impact the markets:
- Wars
- Terrorist Attacks
- Virus Pandemics
- Major Elections in the United States, China, Britain and Japan
- Inflation
- Large Fund Groups selling
- A Major Catastrophe or World Event

This list just highlights why it is impossible to time market entry and how so many of these factors can be playing out at any one time. It also highlights why you need to develop your investment plan and allow the stock market to do its thing and why you are best to take advantage of its momentum and flow with it, rather than try and swim against it!

Chapter 4

Beginner Stock Market Terminology to Know

There are many, many different investing terms that you should learn if you wanted to become an expert in investing in the stock market. This book isn't the 'Expert Guide', rather the 'Beginners Guide' therefore I will try and keep these to the ones that I believe as a starting point you need to know. I certainly don't expect that you will remember them all; it will be just a great reference point if you ever need to refer back when investing in your early trading days.

Common Stock Market Terms

Ask: This is the price per share that people want to get in exchange for their stock.

Bid: This is the price that people are willing to pay for each share to get a stock.

Blue Chip Stocks: The stock/share of a large well-respected, public companies that have a history of steady revenues and dividend payments.

Bond Funds: These funds invest in fixed income instruments such as government bonds and investment-grade or high-yield corporate bonds. These generate an income from interest and have a greater return than money market funds while having less volatility than general stocks.

Broker: An individual or organization facilitating transactions between buyers and sellers of security. Each transaction is charged with a commission, usually on the part of the seller, in exchange for their service. Most stockbrokers provide market research and data for their customers and these days are mostly all online.

Balanced Funds: These funds mix fixed-income and stock securities. This results in a greater potential return than bond funds while decreasing the volatility of stock funds. A balanced fund can lean towards more potential growth by adding more equities in its assets or more conservative risk by allocating more to bonds.

Bull Market: a market where the overall trend is up.

Bear Market: A market where the overall trend is down.

Capitalization: This is how much the market thinks a company is worth.

Capital Gain: The profit when the sale price of a share is higher than the share's cost. This refers to realized gain opposed to unrealized gains which are hypothetical.

Correction: A price move that goes against the recent trend

Day Order: This is an order that only lasts until trading closes for the day.

Day's Range: It refers to the highest and lowest price point that a stock experienced for its all-time record or for a given period.

Day Trader: Someone who trades during the day, but generally closes out trades before the close of the trading day.

Dip: A minor move down in an otherwise strong trend

Dividend: Are a company's distribution of its earnings to its shareholders.

Dividend Reinvestment: An option where a company's existing shareholders can choose to have their cash dividend payments automatically reinvested in additional shares of the company's share

Dividend Yield: The dividend returns to the stockholder in relation to the last quoted sale price. It is calculated by dividing the dividends per stock by the previous sale price, expressed as a percentage.

Earnings Per Share (EPS): A company's net profit divided by the total number of shares in the company.

Exchange: A place wherein different investments, including stocks and bonds, are traded between investors and businesses.

Exchange-Traded Funds (ETFs): These are similar to Index Funds in the fact that these track an Index by holding a combination of securities. But, unlike mutual funds tracking indices, ETFs are easily traded in exchanges through market prices similar to stocks.

Equity: Commonly known as a share or stock.

Growth Stocks: These stocks are expected to have above-average growth compared to the rest of the market.

Hedging: Protecting against limiting losses on an existing share position by establishing an opposite position in the same or equivalent share/stock.

Index Funds: These funds have the objective of tracking the performance of an Index and is a portfolio that resembles the components of the benchmarked Index.

Limit order: It is a conditional order executed when a security reaches a specified price or better. This helps a buyer to ensure that they get in or out of the position at the pre-determined market price of the stock.

Market Order: It is the instruction provided that will be immediately executed at the current market price of a stock. It is always fulfilled as long as willing buyers and sellers are present.

Market Price: This is how much was paid for each share or stock in the latest order executed. This will fluctuate every time the price changes in the market. The market price upon closing the market for the day is the one recorded in the charts.

Market trend: This is the perceived direction of where a market is seen to move in the future.

Margin Call: A call when the amount borrowed in margin lending account exceeds the agreed limit.

Moving Average: It is the average price per share of a stock during a specific timeframe. Common timeframes are in 50 and 200 days.

Mutual Funds: Mutual funds are financial vehicles that consist of pooled funds that are invested in a mixture of financial securities and assets. This could be a combination of stocks, bonds, money market instruments, and more.

Order: This is a bid to buy or sell shares of stock or option contracts.

O.B.V.: On Balance Volume is an indicator or analytical tool that measures the direction of the volume of purchases on any one particular day or period.

Paper-Profit: The theoretical profit that would be made if a trade were closed out at a given price, or at a particular time.

Public Float: This is the number of shares/stocks that a company makes available for trade in the stock market.

Price Chart: The plotting of the prices of a stock on a scale – can be for minutes, a day, a week, monthly or even years.

Quote: This is the latest trading price of a stock. A stock quote is more up-to-date when found in a broker's stock trading platform.

Quote (Buy): This means that you intend to buy shares or take a position in a company's stock.

Quote (Sell): This means that you intend to sell a given number of a company's stock.

Rally (Recovery): Prices moving in an upward direction after a decline.

Range: The difference between the high price and the low price for a given period

Ticker Code: It is an arrangement of characters that serve as a unique identifier for publicly traded stocks. These are also used for indices, options, bonds, and mutual funds. For example, Apple Inc. has a ticker stock of AAPL. Starbucks Corporation has a ticker code of SBUX.

Stock/Company Name: This is the company name but usually abbreviated as a 'Ticker' Code.

Sectors: Allotment of companies into categories. Eg. Energy, Industrial, Banks.

Share: This is a common name that is used by many countries representing ownership of a company and entitling its owner to the right to receive dividends

P/E Ratio: This stands for **P**rice **E**arnings **R**atio. It is calculated by dividing the last sale price by the earnings per share. It, therefore, measures the stock price in relation to the company's profits.

Stop-Loss Order: It is a conditional order executed when a security reaches the indicated price. Once it reaches the indicated price, it becomes a market order. It is designed to limit losses or protect profits incurred from a position.

Stop-Limit Order: It is a conditional order that combines elements of stop-loss and limit order. The order is executed at a specified price within a certain timeframe. But this will only occur when the given stop price occurs in the market.

The stop-limit order provides a trader control on

when the order would be executed. However, it has no guarantee of occurring since the stock may not reach the stop price within the specified timeframe.

Stock Index: It provides a market and performance overview of a section of the stock market. An Index is calculated through the weighted average of a selection of stocks that best represent its section.

Value Stocks: These stocks trade at a market price below what their earnings, sales, and dividends show.

Volatility: The relative amount or percentage by which stock price rises and falls over a period of time.

Volume: The number of shares traded in a given period.

Target Price: This is the price of a stock projected in the future by an investment analyst. The target price is estimated using a combination of analysis of a stock's finances, future supply and demand in the market, fundamentals, and technical data. The target price is the ideal point for some investors and traders to sell their position and realize their gains.

Yield: This is the return on investment received from a stock investment in terms of dividends. This is calculated by dividing the stock's annual dividend amount by the amount paid for its purchase.

Volume 100's: The total number of stocks traded in a particular time period, usually daily. This indicates the level of market interest in a specific stock.

52-week High and Low: The highest and lowest price the stock has traded over the year to date.

Global Markets and Indices to be familiar with:

DOW JONES: The New York Dow Jones Industrial Average (known as the DOW) is the oldest and most widely known and quoted indicator of stock market change. It represents a group of 30 major companies actively traded on the New York Stock Exchange (NYSE).

The NASDAQ: This is also a United States Indicator that measures the successes of the 'new wave' technology companies in the U.S.

The S&P: The S&P 500 Index covers the Top 500 US stocks and is an indicator of the broader U.S. economy.

London's FTSE 100: This is the equivalent of the New York's Dow Jones Index. Its commonly referred to as the 'Footsie'. FTSE stands for Financial Times Stock Exchange (Index)

The Nikkei 300: This is the Index for the Tokyo Stock Exchange and reflects the value of 300 of Japans leading listed companies.

Australia's ASX: This stands for the Australian Stock Exchange.

Chapter 5

Quick Tips to Help You Save For Investing

In this chapter, I will provide you with 7 Great Tips for saving. The reason we want to save money is it allows us to place money aside to be able to invest in our long-term future and stock wealth creation.

T.I.P. 1 – CASH is KING

Whenever possible, use cash or savings via your saving account card to make purchases rather than a Credit Card. A Credit Card is using someone else's money to purchase items that you will end up paying more for through accrued interest. It can be a real money handbrake and debt trap for compulsive shoppers.

T.I.P. 2 – MAKE A LIST and STICK TO IT

Don't treat your trip to the shops as a spending game or leisure activity. Make a list before you leave home and only purchase what is on the list. Remember to think about the value of the item you are buying now and what it may be worth in 2 years. Will the value have increased or decreased?

T.I.P. 3 – IF YOU CAN'T AFFORD IT, DO NOT BUY IT

It is a straightforward tip, but one that is perhaps the one that people overlook more than any! If it requires you to use a Credit Card, it either means you don't have the cash to purchase it, you are not budgeting correctly, or you haven't developed an emergency 'cash-pool' for those unexpected expenses that come up like a broken washing machine that needs replacing.

T.I.P. 4 – EAT OUT LESS AND TAKE YOUR LUNCH

If you were to keep a tab on the amount you spend monthly on eating out, coffee's and buying your lunch, you would be shocked! As you may only be spending $5 – $8 here and there, you don't take much notice. The problem is that when it adds up to $200 per month, that is cash that could be worth well over $500,000 if invested over 20 years. Again, this is my strong argument why automating an investment savings plan is just so important.

T.I.P. 5 – BE PREPARED TO SETTLE FOR SECOND HAND OR GENERIC BRAND TYPES

Many shops, particularly grocery and pharmacy

stores, offer their own' home brand' varieties rather than very well-known brands. What you are likely to find is that they are very close or even equal in quality or effectiveness. You could see yourself spending 20 – 50% less on these generic brands saving yourself a small fortune.

T.I.P. 6 – HAGGLE FOR DISCOUNTS
For many white-goods such as dishwashers, vacuum cleaners and washing machines, you would be amazed at what discount you can get just by merely 'asking'! Many people feel embarrassed to ask if that is the lowest price available and you will find that many stores would prefer to give you a 10% discount than have you go to a competitor.

Another idea is to look up the item for sale via an online store, and when you visit the physical store, they are very likely to have a price-match policy or better the offer by 5% if the brand is identical to what they are selling.

The way I think about asking for discounts is that the savings are better off in your pocket and working for you via investment streams than in the pockets of the big retailers!

T.I.P. 7 – AUTOMATIC SAVINGS PLAN

Work out roughly what you earn every two weeks and then commit to an automatic savings plan of 10%. To do this, there are 4 straightforward steps to create an excellent saving and investment strategy:

- Determine your 10% towards an investment plan. E.g. $250 p/month.
- Jump on your banking APP on your phone and request a new Savings Account called 'My Wealth Building Account.'
- Once established, go to 'Set Up Transfers' and there will be instructions to set up an automatic transfer either weekly, fortnightly or monthly. Choose your cycle and then plug in your amount.
- Once this amount builds to $500 or $1,000, commit to invest that money into wealth-creating investments like Stocks.

We'll have more on this strategy in Chapter Nine.

Chapter 6

How to Invest in Stocks

If you were to do a quick poll on the street to find out what people thought when investing in the Stock Market, the most popular answers would most likely be:

- **Stocks are too risky**
- **I don't know how they work so I don't bother**
- **I don't think about them at all!**

Many people have images from well-known movies with stockbrokers driving expensive cars or with their face buried in their hands when they 'lose it all'. The media also love to build up bad news on front pages of newspapers with '10 Billion wiped from the market in one day'. The only people this should scare are those that are 'Stock Market Players' and those that have a 'get in – get out quickly' kind of mentality. If you are a 'stock investor', you should sleep comfortably that over time, well-chosen stocks have very healthy returns despite the ongoing rises and sometimes dramatic falls of the market.

So, what are stocks?

A stock is a part-ownership of a company that is listed on the stock market. Effectively, when you purchase a stock, you are becoming a very small part-owner of that business. You are taking an equity share in that business. The 'stock' you purchase could be worth $150 per stock or a few cents per stock/share. This price can fluctuate daily depending on the popularity of the stock and number of people buying or selling on a particular day.

How do you make money from stocks?

There are two ways that you can earn money from investing in stocks. Firstly, companies (not all) may pay their stockholders an income stream generally a couple of times per year. This is known as a *dividend*. Dividends may be paid in the form of cash, additional stocks (called a Dividend reinvestment) or sometimes at a discount for the allocation of new shares called 'rights issues'.

If a company that you own stocks in makes a profit, as a part-owner of that stock, you are entitled to share in the growth of that company. The size of your payment will depend on how many stocks of that company you own and the company will allocate a % for every stock you own. For example, if you had 1000 shares in a company, and their dividend is $0.05 per share, you will receive $50. Now there are a number of calculations and tax implications that occur when you do receive a dividend, so I highly recommend you seek financial advice from your accountant regarding taxation on dividends.

In some instances, a company may offer you a 'Dividend Reinvestment Plan'. This means that rather than receiving 'CASH' as a payment, the company will purchase additional stocks for you at a discounted price. Using our $50 example above, rather than receiving $50, the company may offer the opportunity for you to purchase additional stocks for $10.00 (usually $10.45) rather than pay the cash dividend of $50. Therefore, you would be allocated a further five shares, and your portfolio continues to grow and usually free of stockbroking fees. Again, there are different tax implications for what you decide to do so I highly recommend advice that will suit your circumstances.

The *second* way you can grow your investment in stocks is through capital growth. This is when the traded price of your stock rises, generally reflecting the positive growth performance and positive outlook for the company on the stock market. For example, if you purchased a stock at $2.50 per unit and their traded price was to increase to $5.00 per unit, you have doubled the value. If on the other hand, they drop to $1.25, you have halved your money. This also demonstrates the importance of taking your time when choosing your stocks to ensure they will be reliable and robust during all cycles of the market. No stock is immune to price fluctuations, regardless of how big or profitable but choosing long term quality shares helps mitigate significant losses.

When should I purchase stocks?
This is entirely up to the individual, and I know you are looking for the secret investing tip, but generally, you invest when having the money to do so. If you were to hold your money waiting for the market or a particular stock to drop, you may either be waiting a long time, or if there is a big correction in the market, you might be too afraid to invest

thinking that the market could drop even further.

Yes, you may hear plenty of stories of those people that have become rich buying at the bottom and selling at the top. This not only requires considerable mastery and knowledge but, in many instances, plenty of luck! My advice is, don't be a gambler of stocks, be an investor and don't try and time the market.

When should I sell my stocks?
The only time you should sell your stocks is if you are truly in need of the money. Exhaust all cash reserves (not credit cards!) and other options like getting a 2nd job before you consider selling. It is a poor investment strategy to liquidate or sell your stocks too often as you will then rack-up unnecessary fees (think brokerage fees, taxes etc.) and this will erode any profit or dividends that you may have made. Again, I want to reinforce the importance of taking your time to research high-quality stocks with great long-term success because if you choose unknown and highly volatile stocks, the price changes for a novice can be challenging to handle. In many situations, they sell and lose out.

This book is all about advocating strong solid long-term growth and not investing like you were choosing horse #5 at the races.

How do I purchase stocks?
Investing in stocks has become very easy compared to what it used to be in the 1980s and even early 1990s. Previously, you needed to find a stockbroker that you would call and they would act on your behalf to purchase or sell the stocks for you. They could also give you advice on when and what to buy and when to potentially sell. With the arrival of online broking platforms, it has become extremely easy and straight forward.

In most cases, you can create an account for free and in approx. 10 minutes, and you can start buying stocks all over the world. Now as a beginner, I certainly wouldn't advocate in buying international stocks just yet and waiting until you have a solid grasp on your own market.

1. To establish an account, follow these simple steps:
2. Research reputable online broking firms or ask

someone you know who they use to invest in stocks.
3. Have your basic contact details
4. A valid email address
5. Your tax information otherwise you will be paying extra tax if you leave this out.
6. A couple of forms of valid identification. Eg. Passport or drivers' licence.
7. Bank Account Details for where funds will be drawn or deposited too.

How do I invest?

Most of the reputable broking platforms will have online tutorials regarding how to complete your first trade. As a brief shortcut, you would do the following:

1. Log into your account.
2. Enter the details of the company you would like to purchase in the search bar using either the full name or the 'Ticker Code'. For example, if you wanted to purchase Apple inc. Stocks, you would enter AAPL and select the option that appears.
3. Select the BUY as the action

4. Under 'Amount Type' select 'value'. Then enter how much you want to invest.
5. Under 'Order Type', select' market.'
6. Click 'Review Order' to check the details.
7. Click 'Submit'

How many stocks do I have to buy?

Once you have you account established and authorized with an online broker, you can start buying your stocks immediately. There is usually no minimum purchase amount; however, some markets do require a minimum, so just check before making your purchase. From my own personal experience, I always purchase in increments of $1,000, but as a beginner, I think $500 is suitable to get started and gain some experience. How many stocks you can purchase for your $1,000 investment will depend on the per-unit price of the stock you wish to purchase. As an example, company X.Y.Z. Inc has a stock price per unit of $2.00; therefore, you will be able to buy 500 shares + any transaction and brokerage costs.

Trades or your stock purchases are created through the orders entered in the order entry interface of your broker's platform. These orders indicate the stock and number of shares that you want to buy, and the ask or bid price for each share. Once you submit your order online, the broker will facilitate this for you, and you will receive a confirmation certificate electronically. Make sure you store this confirmation certificate safely and somewhere you can access when it comes to tax time Orders will push through when there are matching sell and bid orders in the market and will automatically purchase them for you. They will also send through a confirmation email to confirm the purchase details and when the money will come out (or in if selling) of your account for the trade.

Advice from one of the World's Greatest Investors – Warren Buffett

If you are reading this book, there is no doubt you would know of Warren Buffett. Mr Buffett is a co-founder of Berkshire Hathaway that was established in 1956. Their initial contribution was US$100,000 and is now worth billions of dollars. To put it simply, if you invested $10,000 in 1964, that investment would be worth over US$240 million. As of May 2020, each stock/unit is valued at

$273,975.00! Now, there's an excellent long-term investment if you had made one! Recognize that it is extremely rare for any stock to perform this well, but it does demonstrate the long-term investment brilliance of Warren Buffett and his partner Charlie Munger.

Warren Buffett's investment strategy includes:
Having a diversified portfolio across several market sectors
Thrift and prudence
Thorough analysis and strict investment criteria leading to the selection of quality, undervalued stocks
A very long-term approach to investing, rejecting marking timing strategies and an indifference to the popular market sentiment.

"...be fearful when people are greedy and be greedy when people are fearful".
Warren Buffett

A Sensible and Long-Term Stock Investment Strategy – Dollar Cost Averaging

I have mentioned in early chapters the importance of an 'Automatic Savings Plan' that will automatically build up savings for you in an investment account that you can then use to invest for the long-term. The 2nd element to this is to use an investment strategy called 'dollar cost averaging'. By using this method, you will rule out trying to 'time' the market; instead, invest in regular cycles or intervals so you can also take advantage of any falls in the market.

As an example, if you had your savings automation set-up, of $250 per month, you would know that every two months you would invest the $500 saved into the market regardless of the conditions. The logic behind this strategy is not only simple to implement but creates an excellent disciplined approach to long term wealth creation. It will also average out the cost of the stocks you purchase over the long term no matter if the market is at a high, or has bottomed out. Trying to 'time' the market is, therefore, not even part of the equation or mindset.

There are two ways you could do this. Firstly, you could regularly contribute to a professionally managed stock fund or equivalent, and they will invest it for you and take a small % cut as a fee. This will rule out having to choose a stock if you would rather a professional do this or you don't have an interest in researching different stocks.

The other way is to purchase the stock/s yourself every 2 – 3 months and keep building your portfolio. You may like to consider investing in an **ETF** (Exchange-Traded Fund) that may comprise of the Top 100 traded stocks; therefore, you are adding diversity to your portfolio, rather than the reliance of single stock doing well. I started this way when beginning and to be honest, these stocks have continued to outperform many of the stocks that I chose individually.

D.I.Y. Investing – Reduce the Risk but Compound Your Growth

Most stock investors either do not take the time to analyze financial statements, don't understand them or would prefer to watch grass grow!

Therefore, for many stock investors, the process of picking stocks can become guesswork which on many occasions will inevitably produce sub-optimal results.

If you would like a simple, yet very effective strategy without the guesswork, I would recommend investing in an ETF or also known as a Listed Investment Company (L.I.C.). No, I wouldn't class it as an exciting investment to follow and one that will give you a boost of adrenalin, but it does offer some excellent reasons why you might choose to elect for a low-cost entry point into the stock market, that over the long-term, has a track record of producing some solid returns and passive income.

Reasons why people choose an ETF.

Diversification:
Through buying into an ETF, it can hold up to 100 or more stocks or trusts, and you can create instant diversification. This approach is a tried and tested approach to reducing risk over time.

Low entry costs:
The net returns could be improved substantially over time if you elect to buy an ETF because you will avoid having to pay entry and exit costs if you were to buy or sell each stock individually.

Long Term Gold Bricks:
By choosing to buy an ETF or L.I.C., it is heavily weighted towards profitable industrial stocks and financials, and therefore you could well outperform the Index over time. You are buying into companies that have demonstrated over many years that they can continue to perform both in upturns and downturns in the economy along with providing dividends to their shareholders.

Dividend Reinvestment:
In many ETF holdings, you have the choice to receive dividends or to reinvest the dividends via a 'dividend reinvestment plan', and they will continue to grow your portfolio base. In most instances, a dividend reinvestment plan should not attract brokerage or other transaction costs and thus can be an effective method for your portfolio to compound your wealth.

D.I.Y. – Risk Vs Return

Although I don't advocate for your initial stock investments to be with individual companies, you may be comfortable with risking more to potentially gain more, or on the flip side, lose more! If this is you, I will outline some key strategies you should look for to determine if a company has potential growth.

#1 - Is it Trending Upwards?
By looking at charts of companies, you can get an initial reading on their 'upward' or 'downward' trend patterns. As stocks don't trend in a straight line, they represent more of a heart-rate monitor, and you need to look at the chart over a minimum of 30 – 60 days or even longer. I sometimes look at it over a 12-month period. This will provide me with the initial data that will give a more accurate view of how the stock is tracking. It is just one of many ways you can determine the improvement in the sediment of a stock, but over time, I have found this method to provide some great investments in my portfolio. (*Refer to graph on next page*)

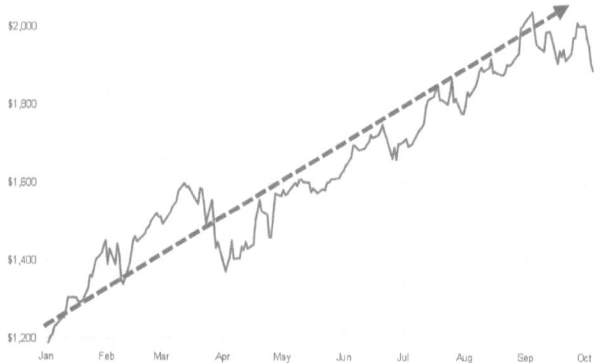

See how there is an upward trend in the stock over an 8-month period

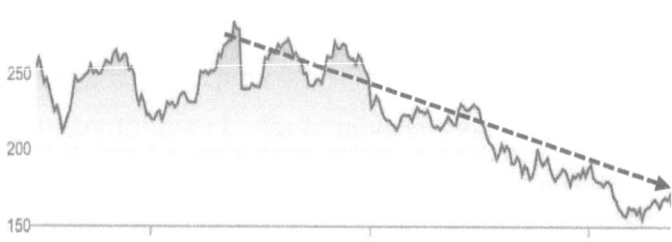

See above an example of a stock that is trending down.

An example of a stagnant stock that looks more like a heart rate monitor

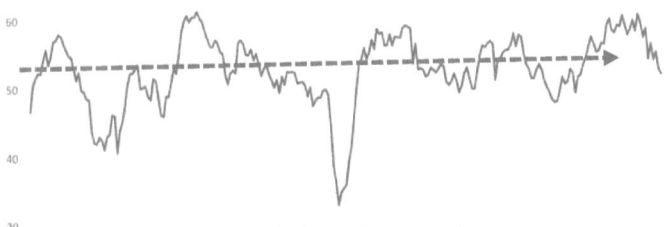

Main Points:
- You will be investing 'blind' unless you look at the chart.
- Look for companies trending up and with a solid timeline.
- Stay clear of the 'stagnant' charts with no upward trend.

#2 – Volume and the Big Guys!

The buying and selling volume of a company is another great indicator to determine if the stock is going to rise or fall in value. There is both 'good' and 'bad' volume, and you get to use the O.B.V. or On-Balance-Volume as a friend.

The O.B.V. will provide an indicator if the big Fund Managers are either buying or selling. This will be very powerful if you want to be buying with the strength of the 'fundies' as they are going to push the prices up.

On the chart below, you will see the 'On Balance Volume' at the bottom of the chart.

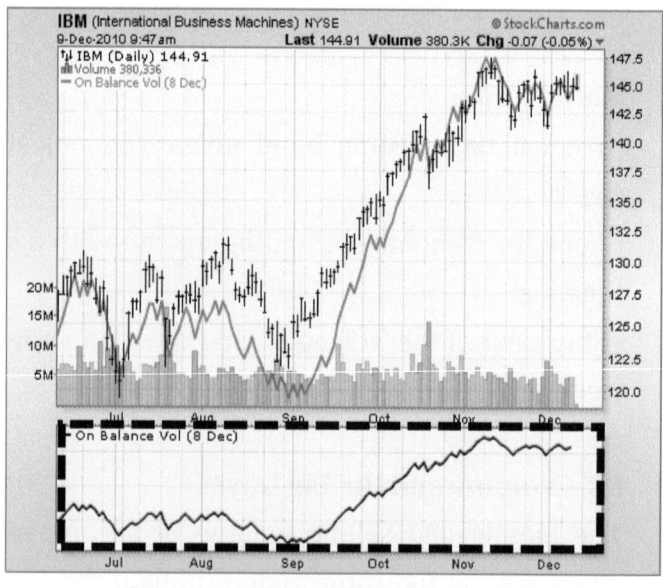

(Source: stockcharts.com)

#3 – The Piglet Buying Strategy

The final tip you can use to accelerate your stock growth is a little riskier but can be beneficial for those that are prepared to study the stock charts and pay closer attention to the movements in the market. I call it the 'Piglet Buying Strategy' because you are feasting when the 'Troughs' appear in the chart.

These opportunities will tie into the trending lines that you create. If you have a solid trend line over a good period of time, as soon as the trending line is broken, you buy-in. For this strategy to be successful, you must be confident that the trend line will continue to move in a northward or upwards direction.

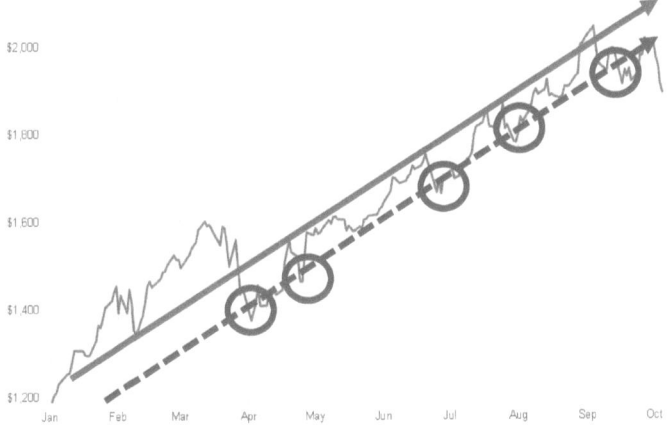

- The Solid Line demonstrates the upward trend of the stock

- The dashed line indicates the 'break and buy' opportunity line.
- The circles indicate the six buying opportunities as the line was broken.

The Safety Net of the Stock-Loss Order

The Stock-Loss Order is the ability to place a 'sell order' in advance of your stock, potentially dropping below a certain price barrier. It's likened to a safety net to protect your gains and reduce the chances of significant losses. Although it does go against the grain of this book in that I want you to think like a long-term investor; I am also acutely aware that I need to provide you with options that enable you to make decisions based on your own unique circumstances.

A Stock-Loss Order can be created via your online broking account under each of your stock holdings. You have the capacity to set the price that you would sell your shares should a time come when the market drops and the price of your stock reaches this threshold.

When would you place a Stop-Loss Order?

- When you know you may be travelling or taken away from your usual day to day schedule.
- When you want to free yourself up from regularly checking the markets
- Prefer automation, so it is a set and forget system.

You can place the order at whatever price you would like, and this can be adjusted at any time you like. If the price of the stock rises, you can lift your Stop-Order to take into consideration the profits that you are making. I mainly use 5% because I never like to lose money, but this is just an individual preference.

Are there any disadvantages from a Stop-Loss Order?

Stop-Loss Orders can be very beneficial for those stocks that have a general 'up-trend' and reduce the chances of significant losses if they lose their momentum. Stop-Loss Orders though can be very difficult to implement on those stocks that have significant volatility.

If you are nervous about significant movements in the market and avoiding potential large losses, then I would certainly recommend you seek financial advice to see if Stop-Loss Orders are suitable for your circumstances and to protect your portfolio.

Do I use my own funds, or should I borrow?

There are several ways that you can purchase stocks, and this could include taking an investment loan to buy your stocks. There could be tax benefits from this strategy, but for now, and until you build your confidence and understanding, I would suggest you keep to the simple and straight forward approach of using your savings for the first 12 months at a minimum. By using your savings to purchase your investments, you rule out going into debt by borrowing for stocks. You will also rule out the 'pressure' that borrowing can cause in the event that the economy turns and your portfolio experiences a downturn. Yes, over the longer term you can investigate if this is a suitable strategy for you, but this is not the book to deep-dive into this, and I want to ensure I keep the information suitable for those just starting on your journey or looking for an approach that is more risk-averse.

Chapter 7

The 7 Rules for Stock Selection for Beginners

Choosing your stocks is a personal choice and one that requires careful consideration, especially if your mindset is that of a one-off purchase that you will remain in your portfolio for a minimum of 10 years or longer if you never need cash quickly.

To help you, I have provided **7 of the Key Rules** that I think you should tick off each time you go to purchase the stock.

Rule 1.
Only invest in companies with a solid performing history.

Does the company have a long history of performing well under a variety of different economic climates and have they consistently paid a stable dividend year after year?

Rule 2.
Do they have strong management?

Are those that are running the company experienced and have a history of producing great results?

Rule 3.
Make a 'BUY' decision with a minimum of 5 years in mind.

By having a long-term focus, you will carefully consider where you place your money, and you will also ignore the gyrations of the market, knowing you have carefully evaluated the business. You will have confidence that the company will continue to grow and be profitable for the long-term.

Rule 4.
Diversification and Balanced Portfolio

Firstly, diversification is ensuring you have an even spread of stocks in your portfolio, as discussed in previous chapters. In other words, don't place all your eggs in the one basket!

When investing in stocks, avoid being waited too heavily into one sector and ensure that the stock you purchase is not more than 5 – 10% of your overall portfolio. Ideally, a portfolio of 5 – 10 stocks across a broad range of industries will provide the diversification you need.

Eg. A Balanced Portfolio of 8 stocks could include:
- 2 Stocks in the **Finance Sector**
- 2 Stocks in the **Technology Sector**
- 2 Stocks in the **Industrial Sector**
- 2 Stocks in the **Energy Sector**
- 2 Stocks in the **Healthcare Sector**

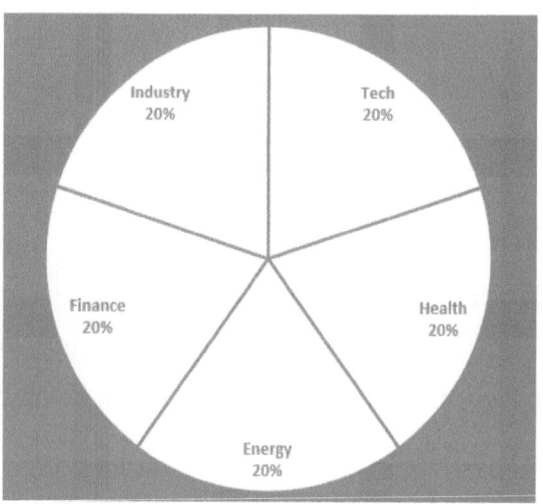

Rule 5.
Learn the Terminology

Some reporting by companies can sometimes blanket the true story of how a company is performing. What can't be glossed over are the data and numbers. As they say, numbers don't lie!

A couple of the most valuable terminologies and information you should learn is Price Earnings (P/E) and Earnings Per Share (EPS). You can find this information on the company website but also on the stockbroking platform you choose under the 'Company Information' section.

If a stock's P/E ratio is higher than the current P/E ratio in the market, the stock is considered trading at or above its current value. But this does not automatically make the stock a bad investment, especially if it is a low-cap stock with a rapid rate of growth. On the other hand, if it is lower than the market's P/E ratio, it is currently trading below value, which makes it a potential value stock.

Rule 6.
Invest in companies you understand

I'm always surprised by how many people invest in companies that they wouldn't be able to explain what they do! If you are unable to explain what a company does in 2 or 3 sentences, chances are you don't know the company well enough.

The best companies to commence your investment journey on, are those that you can physically touch the products or walk into their stores or use their equipment, services or resources. If you or people you know don't use them, why would anyone else? This rule stops you looking to purchase 'the next big thing' and makes you focus on the customer end experience and why they may have been performing so well for so many years.

Rule 7.
Stick to Your Wealth Creation Plan

Once you have developed your investment strategy and plan, stick with it. The best investors and those that generate the best passive income are those that have remained with their long-term investment strategy and continued regardless of the movements of the market. Should you identify that your plan isn't working, then STOP, REVIEW what is going wrong, PIVOT and change direction if necessary and then POWER on and continue on your journey.

Chapter 8

Investment Automation and Wealth Acceleration

Why is automation a great investing tool?

The process of automation in many aspects of our lives has simplified and also sped up the way we do things. The definition of 'Automation' is "the technique, method, or system of operating or controlling a process by highly automatic means, as by electronic devices, reducing human intervention to a minimum" (dictionary.com). 'Reducing the human intervention to a minimum' is the key to this process and why using its convenient functionality with our stock marking investing system is so beneficial.

Many people feel that if they automate, they lose control, but I disagree. Automating a process that has a sound system and structure will remove many of the emotional aspects of stock investing that causes many to make irrational short-term decisions that will have long-term financial impacts. The process of automation comes into its own when we can use historical data and information to develop automations that we can have confidence will work both in upturns and downturns in the market.

Historically, we know that over time, the Index continues to surge ahead following significant events and stock crashes. As an example, if someone had invested $10,000 on January 1st 1970 in the Vanguard Index fund, that investment would now be worth just under $2 million in 2020. That's an annual year by year increase of 11.4% p.a

Although we are unable to determine what future markets will do, the historical data continues to indicate that markets do rebound to even greater heights following significant crashes in the market. It is due to these crashes that having an automation system in place stops your emotions from making decisions and allowing the automated system to make them on your behalf. This permits the compounding effect to work its magic.

Why do compounding and automation work so well in partnership?

Compounding, upon first glance, may not initially make any logical sense. How could $100,000 in Year 1, turn into $800,000 in year 21? How can your investment double every 7 years? As an example, see below what occurs if an investment were to rise by an average of 10% p.a and from year 35 to 42, the portfolio has a gain of $3.2 million, therefore exceeding the gains of all of the previous 35 years of $3.1 million.

YEAR	PORTFOLIO ($)
0	100,000
7	200,000
14	400,000
21	800,000
28	1,600,000
35	3,200,000
42	6,400,000

You can draw a few conclusions from this table and the compounding impact.

1. The early you start investing, the better.
2. Invest in assets like quality stocks where you never have to sell them.
3. This demonstrates that the later you start, the more difficult it is to play catch-up due to the compound snowball effect.
4. If you purchased and sold stocks to often, you

may miss out on the average 10% returns that Index Fund stocks have historically generated.
5. Time: Allow your portfolio to work and don't fall for the trap of expecting immediate results with your portfolio.

A greater reason why compounding and automation work so well in a partnership is because people can be terrible at saving money to invest. When an automatic stock investment strategy is built, which I will show you shortly how to do, you can use the set & forget strategy to compound your gains. If someone is very good at saving, this money may also be used to purchase depreciating items like cars if the money is left too long without 'working for you'.

How to establish your own 'Automatic Stock Building Wealth System'.

In his book 'Automatic Millionaire', David Bach tells the story of Jim and Sue McIntyre, a couple that became millionaires off a very modest income by establishing a 'pay yourself first' system. He explained how they invested 10% of their income immediately when they got paid and before they could touch or spend it, month in, month out for more than 30 years. They started conservatively at 4%, and then slowly built it to 5%, then 6% and all the way to 10%. After several years, they increased it to 15% because they became used to living off the same income. Every time they received an increase in salary, they just increased their investment strategy by the % of that increase.

Using this strategy, let's now look at the 5 steps to invest in stocks using an automation system.

Step 1.
Establish your Stock Investment Account

As briefly discussed in Chapter 6, to begin your strategy, you need to establish a separate bank account that you may like to call your 'Stock Investment Account'. This account will be used 'only' to save and accrue money for investing and is only accessed either via automatic withdrawals for investing or at intervals to purchase stocks via the dollar cost averaging method. This account may also be the account you established when creating your online broker account for all of your stock transactions.

Step 2.
Decide how much you will 'Pay Yourself First.'
Next, decide what dollar amount of your pay you will allocate to your stock investment account the moment you get paid and before you can spend it. Eg. $80 per week or $320 p/month.

Step 3.
Set-up the automatic transfer online with your bank
Log into your account and set-up the automatic transfer to occur each payday. If you get paid fortnightly, set it up for the day of pay, likewise if you get paid monthly. For the self-employed, you need to do the same thing, with your most significant challenge being regular and consistent cash flow to work-around.

Step 4.
Accumulation and Periodical Investments
This step requires the most disciplined action because it will require you for every investment cycle to invest your accumulated amount into your chosen stock/s. You will use the dollar cost average system and invest regardless of what cycle the

market is moving through. If you have just the one stock, eg. ETF (Exchange-Traded Fund) that you invest in, this will be a straightforward process. Just log onto your stock platform, calculate the number of shares/stocks you can purchase for your accumulated funds using the tool they provide when buying, while also taking into account any transaction costs to purchase your stocks.

Step 5.
Diarize for your next investment cycle

It may be a great idea to diarize in your calendar each investment cycle. For example, you may like to invest on the first Monday of each quarter. Again, it is all about spending just 15 minutes to establish the automation and then set and forget.

The beauty of this system is that it may take you 1 hour to initially establish, and then just 10 minutes each 3 months to log in and purchase your stocks. Over the year, it may only equate to 1 hour of your time to automate an excellent investment strategy and allow compounding to play a huge part in building your portfolio.

Chapter 9

Stock Market Mistakes Beginners Make

Making mistakes is part of any journey you embark on, but it is usually the financial mistakes that tend to haunt you for a little longer. As a beginner investor, there will be some mistakes you make and therefore, the information and tips in this quick guide will avoid many costly ones.

Undoubtedly, many novice stock investors still make repeated mistakes like many before them, so here are seven mistakes that beginners do make. The most crucial step to avoid these mistakes is being aware of them and avoid making the same errors of judgement.

Mistake No. 1 - They invest in 'Hot Stock Tips.'
As beginners, we all dream that our first stock will make us into a millionaire in 4 weeks. Sadly, this will not be the case for 99.99% of beginner investors. Perhaps over many years, the stock could if you remain firm with your wealth creation strategy.

Many starting out listen and take advice from hot tips from stock market forums or family functions. It could be a tip about the next 'Uber' that will become a huge success story or a mining company about to hit the 'Lithium' jackpot. So many beginners make these very costly mistakes, and you need to keep your 'radar' on all the time.

Mistake No. 2 - Poor Preparation

Investing in shares/stocks has to be treated like a family-owned and operated business. You need to prepare, plan and have your wealth creation strategy firmly in place. Start small and build incrementally, learning from each of the stocks you buy.

Mistake No. 3 – Remaining strong emotionally

Many beginners get caught up in the 'if I don't buy now, I might miss out' emotional rollercoaster. If you begin to feel this way, you need to step away and use the 'dollar-cost-average' approach. This way, you will invest at cyclical times rather the trying to time the market. If you develop the 'Fear of Missing Out' as an investment strategy, I'm very confident that you will always miss out and lose most of your money.

The often-repeated mistake that beginners make is selling when they see their stock starting to fall. Have an interest in your stock performance but don't judge its performance over hours, days or weeks, judge it over many months and years. If you do find yourself checking your portfolio too often, move the APP or create a greater resistance so you stop checking frequently.

Mistake No. 4 - They second guess their stock choices.

Most beginners are nervous when they purchase their stocks as they are unsure if they have made the right decision. This is entirely understandable. What you need to do is check your stocks periodically rather than their performance daily. To do this, set up a calendar reminder to occur once per week or once per fortnight. You may even be comfortable setting it to once per/month.

If you feel that you want to 'dip your toe' into stock investing slowly, then purchasing an ETF (Exchange Traded Fund) as you can buy ETF's that comprise of 50, 100 or even 200 of the Top Traded Companies in your respective market. This way, you will have the diversification and the benefit being that any changes in one company will not significantly impact your entire portfolio.

Mistake No. 5 – They treat it like a game

Long-term wealth creation is not a game. You need to treat it with respect and never 'gamble' away your money. Many beginners jump into stocks looking for a quick win or believe they have the uncanny ability to always purchase shares that will be winners in the short term. From my experience, this kind of attitude will often lend itself to poor choices and overall disappointment.

Mistake No. 6 – Poor Accounting

Do not undervalue the importance of knowing your numbers. Many platforms offer the convenience of collating your TAX reporting information from your stock portfolio so you can complete your tax returns. Just ensure you have an organized approach and keep all documentation related to your investments secure and easy to reference when required.

Mistake No. 7 – They don't give it time

Many beginners purchase their first parcel of stocks, see it fall the next day and think about selling them! This is why your research and overall strategy needs to be robust and free emotionally of the short-term rises and falls of the stock. Know when buying that you have a 50% chance that your stock could fall either on the same day you purchase, or even the following day. None of us knows what will happen from one day to the next. Therefore, it reinforces why researching and understanding your purchase plan is just so critical, regardless of your experience as a stock investor.

Chapter 10

21 Great Money Tips to Grow Your Wealth and Passive Income

In this chapter, I am going to provide you with 21 Money Tips that will help you dramatically increase your wealth and build a solid foundation for your overall financial success. Importantly, building up your wealth is a process of life-long learning, and therefore, your starting position should be to learn as much as you can. Remember, your money success depends on it!

1. Start as early as you can. Allow the magic of compounding to work to your favour.
2. Allocate 10% of what you earn to invest in your future.
3. Avoid Credit Cards. Use cash or a Debit Card.
4. Invest in the long-term. On average, stocks rise 10% over a decade.
5. Develop a diversified portfolio of great stocks in different sectors
6. Learn to buy when people are fearful and hold when people are greedy (W. Buffett)
7. Invest in companies that you as a customer buy yourself
8. Use the dollar-cost averaging purchase plan and ignore the gyrations of the market.

9. Don't become emotional and look at the daily up's & downs of the market.
10. Avoid at all costs 'Hot Tips'. Do your homework
11. Once you become more experienced, consider international stocks for diversity.
12. Start small and build incrementally in parcels of $1,000 per transaction. More if your savings budget permits.
13. Research, Research and Research more. You would rather take the time to choose a great stock that offers great value than to rush and spend a lifetime lamenting on your decision on a very poor performing stock.
14. It is essential to have a plan to commit to your wealth-building strategy. Any plan is better than no plan at all.
15. In the beginning, review your plan after three months, then six months and then annually.
16. Beginning investors should consider investing in an ETF. An ETF will diversify your investment across many companies rather than just one. As you grow confidence, you can then expand your

portfolio to contain other individual companies.
17. Be prepared to purchase 2nd hand goods. They will save you a fortune.
18. Limit those purchases that are depreciating assets.
19. Learn from the best investors in the world like Warren Buffett.
20. Seek financial counsel where needed. It will cost you money if you don't!
21. Establish an automatic saving and investment system. What you don't see in your account, you won't miss.

Chapter 11

Developing Your Stock Investment Plan

In this final chapter, it is essential that we now develop our simple plan of action to begin investing in the stock market. You can have a very bright and exciting financial future ahead, and the process begins today to ensure you have the plan and strategy in place that will enable you to build a passive income stream that will provide income during the day and also while you sleep.

The initial key is taking action and implementing what you have learnt from this book so you can benefit financially moving forward. To assist you in establishing this plan, here are several initial questions and goals you can develop to create your momentum for investing in the stock market by using this template.

YOUR WEALTH PLAN

Top 3 Stock Investment Goals for the next 12 Months

1.
2.
3.

Next 5 Steps I will take to start or continue my stock investment journey

1.
2.
3.
4.
5.

Available Funds: $_____

Monthly amount you will automate and invest in stocks: $_____

Current size of Stock Portfolio: $_____

As of (enter date) _____/_____/_____

Investment cycle eg. January, April, July, October

Month_____

Date_____/_____/_____

Month_____

Date_____/_____/_____

Month_____

Date_____/_____/_____

Month_____

Date_____/_____/_____

Knowledge Expansion

How many books will you read in 12 months on investing? _____

What further training will you do to improve your stock investment knowledge?

_____

_____

_____

_____

Starting 5 Point Checklist Plan

- ☐ I have my Stock Goals written down
- ☐ I have developed my stock investment strategy
- ☐ I have a 12-month plan developed for stock market investing
- ☐ I have identified ways I can save for investing
- ☐ I have established my automated investment structure

Many people will be keen to skip over the initial planning and goal setting stage for Stock Investing. I can't emphasize enough the importance of mapping out your long-term plan and knowing what your long-term goals are. The template I have provided will provide an initial framework for a start, although you should aim to spend a good number of hours by yourself or with the support of a Financial Planner creating a tailored plan that is just right for you.

To download your own free planning template, please visit:
https://thelifegraduate8265.activehosted.com/f/19

Conclusion

Throughout this book, many tips have been highlighted to get your investment journey started. There are seven habits that I must highlight that if you forgot everything else, would position you very well.

Habit No #1

Know exactly what it is that you want out of investing. Describe your goals. Write them down because they can't just remain in your head. Make sure you see them every day. Once you've described them (e.g. a nice home, a four-week holiday each year, a holiday home and to retire with enough to give you a comfortable independent life), then quantify what you need to save and regularly invest in making all this happen. You need to know the amount you can periodically earmark for stock investing, while realizing there will be windfall events or chaos happenings that can derail your plans but, eventually, the agreed plan will reassert itself.

Habit No #2

Avoid 'get rich schemes' or promises of great wealth in dubious start-ups. Know what the company you invest in does and test your knowledge by explaining it to a family member or friend. Investors need to identify quality companies, putting their longer view on investing together with their understanding of what a quality company/asset means, they can follow the advice of Warren Buffett who has advised: "Be fearful when others are greedy. Be greedy when others are fearful." You become an 'outside the square' investor because you buy when others are selling and because you know what constitutes a quality asset.

Habit No #3

You develop an investment strategy that suits who you are when it comes to risk. This strategy has to be linked to your goals, and there can't be a disconnect, or your dreams will never come true. When young people ask me for guidance, I suggest being fully invested in stocks. It is sensible because there will be many ups and downs in their lifetime, but the upward trend of stocks is persistent over time.

Habit No #4

Investing isn't punting — it's investing in assets that you hope will rise in value and probably pay you income. A quality share/stock that rises in value and pays income or dividends can be like a quality investment property that rises in value over time and pays income or rent. You must dedicate yourself to become an expert on investing, so you know the difference between speculation (punting) and putting your money to work into a quality share/company that will help you grow your wealth. It's an attitude thing where you progress over time from being an amateur investor to eventually becoming a very confident and successful one. Investing and wealth-building is an aspirational activity, and you have to be up for self-improvement and be committed to learn about all the things that a pro knows. It means you need to understand risk, diversification, reweighting your portfolio, dollar-cost averaging and so on.

Habit #5

Invest regularly and stick to your investment cycle.

Habit #6

Automate your investments where you can. Take the emotion out of the purchase with dollar cost average 'BUYS'.

Habit No #7

Don't ever fall into the trap of never enjoying your money. Yes, we need to create a budget, save for investments but also plan to allocate some money that you can enjoy. Making more money will offer up the opportunity for more choices and how you spend your life. By building up your wealth slowly in stocks now, you will enjoy so much more freedom than you ever thought possible later on.

Remember, there are many different ways you can invest, and the choice will ultimately be yours on what you feel most comfortable with. Stocks have the benefit of liquidity, and if you ever needed cash in an emergency, you can have your money in your account in a few days. Property chosen well is also an excellent vehicle to grow your wealth. However, you have many more things to consider like tenants, insurance, purchasing and selling costs and potentially very long selling timelines should you need to get the money. Remember, you can't sell half a house to get some money, but you can sell half your shareholding if you needed to!

Although this book is roughly a 60 to 90-minute guide into the world of investing, we have covered some great starting elements. To refresh you, these have included:

- **The 7 money guiding steps for building wealth and how to develop the right mindset**

- **Establish your financial goals through the 8-step process**

- **The basic financial terminology you should know to get started**

- **The 7 quick tips to help you save for investing**

- **A quick guide on how to invest in stocks**

- **The 7 beginner rules you should know for stock selection**

- **How to establish an automatic stock purchase plan**

- **The common mistakes that beginners make**

- **21 money tips for growing your wealth & passive income**

- **7 habits for great stock investing**

Your wealth building in stocks starts with a plan and begins today by Taking Action. You have the template to start, the necessary knowledge to establish an account, and the plan for all your financial goals and dreams to be achieved. You are now on the starting grid, and it is now time to enter the world of the stock market!

PLEASE LEAVE A REVIEW

I would greatly appreciate if you enjoyed this book to please leave a review. Your review will assist the book to reach more people and have a positive impact on their lives. Think of it as your gift back to me!

Resources

1. *Bach.D, The Automatic Millionaire, 2005,*
2. *Town.P, Payback Time, 2009,*
3. *Scollon. T, Fair Share, 2005,*
4. *Wargent. P, Take a Financial Leap, 2015,*
5. *Clitheroe. P, Making Money, 2004,*
6. *Switzer. P, Join the Rich Club, 2019*
7. dictionary.com

www.ingramcontent.com/pod-product-compliance
Ingram Content Group UK Ltd.
Pitfield, Milton Keynes, MK11 3LW, UK
UKHW042001230426
12048UKWH00009B/461